In Praise of P

"From the first checkbox, Lisa Schab pulls the emotionally overwrought person of any age into a workbook that is inventive, lively, and profoundly useful. Structurally and visually, this engaging book brings emotional skills to life, using sensory, physical, spiritual, and analytic approaches. The format is bite-sized, fast-paced, and appealing—even for teens—but the ideas communicated are life-changing. Using writing and creativity, the reader naturally develops tools that demystify the often difficult world of emotions. I facilitate writing groups for teens, and the exercises in *Put Your Feelings Here* will be a welcome addition."

> —BETH JACOBS, PhD, author of *Writing for Emotional Balance, The Original Buddhist Psychology*, and *A Buddhist Journal*

"Lisa Schab has done a brilliant job teaching some of the dialectical behavior therapy (DBT) skills in a fun, creative, and understandable way to help teens manage their emotions. I love it!"

> —SHERI VAN DIJK, MSW, psychotherapist, international speaker, and author of several DBT books, including *Don't Let Your Emotions Run Your Life for Teens*

"This is an excellent book for teens struggling with anxiety. It combines journaling and DBT skills into a particularly helpful tool for adolescents who struggle with low stress tolerance and high emotionality. With more than one hundred exercises, each has a purpose and meaning; they don't just busy the reader, but rather enhance the reader's understanding of their emotions and the necessity to manage them.... I highly recommend this book."

> —DEB NORTON, MS, LCPC, NCC, private practice therapist specializing in adolescent psychology

"*Put Your Feelings Here* is a creative way for making teens place their emotions on paper. I like that it teaches me skills that I can use in everyday life in similar situations. I like that the book mainly uses visual exercises because not everyone can put what they are feeling down in writing in a few simple words. I liked its humor. I liked how it did not just help you cope with problems, but help solve the problems. I would recommend the book."

—BEE, Chicago, IL; graduated eighth grade;
entering high school in fall 2019 for visual arts

"Lisa Schab's *Put Your Feelings Here* is an easy-to-use tool accessible to teenagers with any level of therapeutic experience. This book empowers teens to build internal awareness, increase emotional intelligence, and practice evidence-based coping skills creatively. *Put Your Feelings Here* makes DBT skills relevant and accessible to today's teens. This book walks the middle path between free journaling and directed prompting, allowing teens to feel in control of the process and to learn transferable skills."

—MARGARET LEWIS, LCSW, associate director
of the Adolescent School Refusal Partial
Hospitalization Program at Compass Health
Center in Northbrook, IL

"Schab expertly weaves together mindfulness, externalization, calm acceptance, and breakthrough change in this rich array of exercises. Equally useful for self-guided work by teens, and directed exercises or homework by therapists. A wonderful addition to the tool chest!"

—LARRY WILSON, MSW, LSW, career counselor at
Wilson Consulting, and former youth counselor

Put Your Feelings Here

A Creative DBT Journal for
Teens with Intense Emotions

Lisa M. Schab, LCSW

INSTANT HELP BOOKS

An Imprint of New Harbinger Publications, Inc.

Publisher's Note

This publication is designed to provide accurate and authoritative information in regard to the subject matter covered. It is sold with the understanding that the publisher is not engaged in rendering psychological, financial, legal, or other professional services. If expert assistance or counseling is needed, the services of a competent professional should be sought.

Distributed in Canada by Raincoast Books

          Instant Help Books
          An imprint of New Harbinger Publications, Inc.
          5674 Shattuck Avenue
          Oakland, CA 94609
          www.newharbinger.com

Cover and interior design by Amy Shoup

Acquired by Tesilya Hanauer

Printed in China

Library of Congress Cataloging-in-Publication Data
on file with publisher

ISBN: 978-1-68403-423-9

22   21

10   9   8   7   6   5   4   3   2

This book is dedicated
with love and joy to every
teen who opens it! May
you find at least one
spark of peace, hope, or
inspiration in these pages.
And may you realize how
beautiful you are.

START HERE

— A VERY BRIEF SURVEY —

1. ☐ I am a robot   ☐ I am a human
(Check the box that applies to you.)

Okay, IF you checked that you are a robot, give this book away right now. You will have no need for it since robots don't have emotions.

IF you checked that you are a human, READ ON, because ALL humans have emotions and ALL humans can use some tips on managing them.

2. ☐ I am a teenager—or in the near vicinity.

☐ I am not a teenager—or anywhere close.
(Check the box that applies to you.)

IF you checked that you're a teen—or close—there's a good chance you not only have emotions, but you also have BIG emotions, somewhat often, and sometimes more than one at a time. You may also swing between one and another fairly quickly.＊

IF you checked you are not a teen—it's still very likely that sometimes your average human emotions can feel out of control. (Because while emotions are totally normal, they can also be tricky and surprising.)

＊This is because during the teen years your body, brain, and hormones are going through *more growing and changing* than at any other time in your life. These changes can cause your average human emotions to feel BIGGER, or *more intense*, than usual, and sometimes <u>overwhelming</u>.

FEELINGS 101

1. There are many different human emotions. (This list is just a sample.) Circle any you're feeling now. Star any you've ever felt.

abandoned	frantic	left out	shy
angry	free	mad	silly
annoyed	frustrated	miserable	shocked
anxious	glad	melancholy	sexy
apprehensive	gratified	nervous	stunned
betrayed	guilty	nice	trapped
brave	grief	nutty	troubled
confused	happy	outraged	uneasy
crushed	hateful	over- whelmed	unsettled
calm	helpless	panicked	upset
cheerful	hurt	peaceful	vivacious
confused	hysterical	pleasant	vulnerable
defeated	intimidated	pressured	wonderful
delighted	infuriated	proud	worried
doubtful	inspired	rejected	Or? . . .
empty	jealous	refreshed	
eager	jumpy	relaxed	
excited	joyful	relieved	
exasperated	lazy	restless	
exhausted	lonely	sad	
fearful	loving	scared	
foolish	lustful		

2. Despite what well-meaning people may have told you, **there are no feelings that are wrong or bad or that you shouldn't feel.** (What you DO with those feelings can have positive or negative consequences!) But, in and of themselves . . .

ALL FEELINGS ARE OKAY.

(You might want to underline or trace over this statement a few times.)

3. You can learn ways to regulate and reduce intense emotions to make them more manageable. This book is designed specifically to help you do that.

SOME THINGS TO KNOW ABOUT THIS BOOK

* It is filled with "prompts," or suggestions for activities that will help you reduce your feelings of intense emotion in the moment.

* It's yours to do in whatever way works best for you. So, you can do exactly what a prompt suggests, or you can change it up. (For example, if it says, "write," and you'd rather draw, you can draw instead. If you have a lot you want to express and there's not enough room, you can tape in some more paper. If it doesn't say, "Cut the edges of these pages into curlicues," but you'd like to cut the edges of the pages into curlicues, go right ahead.) Also, you can do these prompts in the order they appear, or in whatever order you want. Regulating emotions is about finding safe ways to calm down, so be guided by what helps you do this the best.

* This is not school. There are no grades, no one is evaluating your self-expressions, and there's no wrong way to do anything in here. So don't worry about how your answers look or sound; just let yourself put what you need to on the paper.

* Some prompts talk about *Emotional, Logical, and Wise Minds.* Here's what that means:

Emotional Mind is the part of your brain that cares only about feelings. It wants you to scream, laugh, and cry without thinking, and to get so caught up in emotion that you might feel like you're drowning. ("Aaarrgghhh, I'm falling apart!")

Logical Mind totally ignores emotions. It wants you to act only on facts, and to forget completely about how you feel. ("There's no reason to feel upset. Just get on with your life.")

Wise Mind takes the middle path, and recognizes the importance of both emotion and logic. It helps you consider both and then make the smartest choice about how to act. ("Of course you're upset; that's okay. Take some time to understand and express your feelings, and then let's plan for how to make things better.") ***Using Wise Mind is generally the healthiest way to help yourself regulate emotions.***

* Some prompts talk about "mindfulness." Mindfulness means focusing your attention on whatever's happening in the present moment, and not judging it. (Research shows that when we're too focused on regrets of the past or worries about the future, it's a lot harder to manage our emotions.) So mindfulness can be a really helpful tool for calming down.

"DBT" is in the subtitle of this book—but what does it mean?? Vote for your choice:

A. **D**ream **B**ig **T**oday: a professional system of wish fulfillment

B. **D**o **B**e **T**rue: a soon-to-be-released country-western hit

C. **D**ialectical **B**ehavioral **T**herapy: a tried-and-true, research-based method for managing big emotions

(The "real" answer is C. But feel free to write about your wishes, or a country-western hit! Writing is a great way to express yourself and your feelings, so just let yourself relax and let your pen fly...)

ANOTHER IMPORTANT NOTE: The purpose of this book is to help you *reduce* intense emotions. If any prompt *increases* your emotional intensity, just notice that. Then take a break or switch to a different prompt. You can try it again later if you want to—or not. You decide.

YOU MIGHT WANT TO TRY THIS

Rate and record the level of your emotional intensity on a 1 (low) to 10 (high) scale right before and right after you do a prompt. Then compare your numbers. This can help you learn what kinds of activities help you most with regulating emotion.

Prompt Page #	Emotional Intensity Before Prompt (1–10)	Emotional Intensity After Prompt (1–10)	Higher? Lower?	By How Much?

YOUR FIRST THOUGHTS
AND FEELINGS

(Write any thoughts or feelings you have about starting
this book.)

What are you feeling right now?

sadness

joy

disgust

FEAR

ANGER

LOVE

ENVY

SURPRISE

Let it out all over these pages.

guilt

Color this page. Breathe slowly and deeply.
(Stay in the lines . . . or don't . . .)

ALL

FEELINGS

ARE

OKAY

Which of your thoughts have your brain's alarm
system jammed on ≋ Red Alert? ≋

_____

_____

_____

_____

Choose any of these calming thoughts to
disarm it now. (Or write your own.)

"I can handle this."

_____

"Everything will work out in time."

"It's going to be okay."

"When I calm down it won't feel so overwhelming."

"It's actually not as bad as it feels."

"If I look at it differently, it doesn't look so bad."

♪♫ Play a song that soothes you. Close your eyes . . .
hear each note . . . become the notes. Draw yourself as music. . .

♩ ♫ ♩ ♪ 17

WHAT WOULD YOUR **EMOTION** LOOK LIKE
IN **PHYSICAL FORM?**

DRAW IT HERE. LEAVE IT HERE.

You're hiking at twilight and come across a Wise Being who's been waiting to give you a message.

What is the Being like?
What is its message?

fire alarm

motorcycle

drums

barking dog

crunching chips

---

friend's voice

---

lullaby

---

whisper

---

drifting feathers

Take a breath and turn down your volume.

When emotions peak, things feel worse than they actually are.
When they plateau again, we see more clearly. Tell both stories:

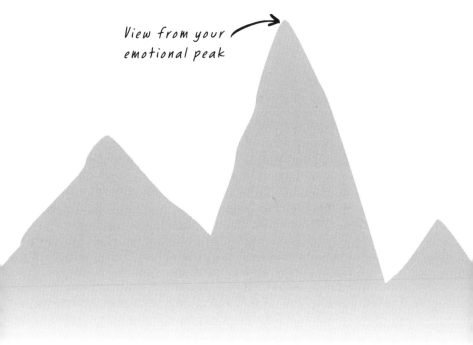

View from your
emotional peak

View from your calm plateau

Describe your COMFORT ZONE.

Shoes off?

Sweats on?

Furry pet?

Big pillows?

Earbuds in?

Warm drink?

Soft blanket?

Or...?

Take yourself there now.

Mixed, jumbled thoughts can raise emotional heat.
Label your current thoughts
to prevent a boilover.

PLANNING (I will . . .)

* _____

_____

_____

_____

JUDGING (That's too . . . I'm too . . .)

* _____

_____

_____

REGRET (I wish I had . . .)

* _____

_____

_____

DESIRE (I'd like . . .)

✳ _____

_____

_____

_____

WORRYING (What if . . .)

✳ _____

_____

_____

_____

HOPE (It's possible that . . .)

✳ _____

_____

_____

_____

Highlight your hopes!

Close your eyes and imagine yourself at the top of a mountain. A gentle rain begins and your emotion is washed off of you.

It runs down your arms, your chest, your legs—down the mountain in rivulets,

Watch your feelings being carried away until the river empties into the sea. How do you feel now?

collecting into streams, running into a river.

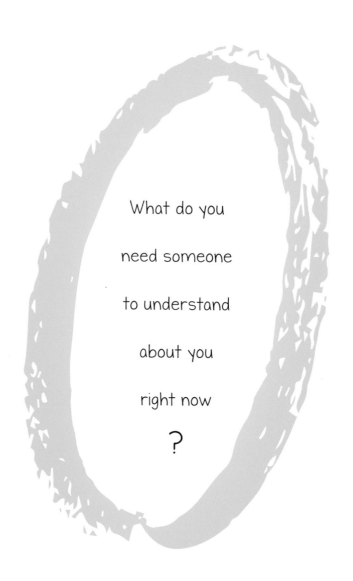

What do you

need someone

to understand

about you

right now

?

Share these thoughts with
someone you trust.

FOCUS SHIFT!
Are you one of the rare people who can:

1. Hum while holding your nose?
___ yes   ___ no   ___ maybe so

2. Draw the number 6 while making clockwise circles with your leg?
___ yes   ___ no   ___ maybe so

3. Touch your tongue to your nose?
___ yes   ___ no   ___ maybe so

4. Tickle yourself?
___ yes   ___ no   ___ maybe so

5. Talk while inhaling through your nose?
___ yes   ___ no   ___ maybe so

6. Wiggle your ears?

___ yes   ___ no   ___ maybe so

7. Put your fist in your mouth?

___ yes   ___ no   ___ maybe so

8. Raise only one eyebrow?

___ yes   ___ no   ___ maybe so

Or?

9. _____

_____

___ yes   ___ no   ___ maybe so

10. _____

_____

___ yes   ___ no   ___ maybe so

Color . . . design . . .
words . . . line . . .
Just fill it in.

A time when you felt the opposite of how you feel right now:

situation • time • day • place • weather

people present ● your thoughts

your actions ● your feelings

Get physical!

run, walk, swim
shoot hoops, weightlift
do yoga
play tennis
play baseball
play lacrosse
play soccer
kickbox
practice martial arts
ski, surf, hike, bike
rappel
kayak, canoe
stretch
play volleyball
or
_____

What happens to the emotion you
were holding in your body?

You're making yourself an emotional Soothie.
What ingredients will you put in?

patience?

positivity?

clear thinking?

forgiveness?

love?

43

EMOTION DOC'S NOTES:

Diagnosis: (name of current emotion)

Cause: (thoughts that brought it on)

Avoid these: (thoughts that will make it worse)

Prescription: (thoughts that can make it better)

"PAIN IS TO BE USED
AS A STEPPING-STONE,
NOT A CAMPGROUND."

—Alan Cohen

Poke holes in this
page with wild abandon!
Let any leftover emotion seep
through and float away.

PUT A COLOR THAT SOOTHES YOU HERE.

Sit quietly and gaze into the space. As you gently inhale and exhale,
imagine this color filling your whole body, mind, and spirit.

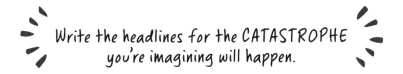

Write the headlines for the CATASTROPHE
you're imagining will happen.

Then write the story of what's <u>more likely to happen</u>.

DRAW OR DESCRIBE YOUR FEELING
AS IF IT WERE . . .

an animal...

a color . . .

a food . . .

music . . .

a natural wonder . . .

A friend texts you exactly what you need to hear right now to help you calm down. **What do they say?**

Take this journal for
a walk outside.

Breathe in the fresh
air until your big
emotions feel smaller.

Show a map
of your trip . . .
Note where your
feelings changed
along the way.

I **can't** change _____

_____

but I **can** choose to think _____

_____

I **can't** change _____

_____

but I **can** choose to think _____

_____

I **can't** change _____

_____

but I **can** choose to think _____

_____

--- FOR EXAMPLE ---

I **can't** change _that I broke my arm._

but I **can** choose to think _it's something that will heal._

I **can't** change _my best friend is moving._

but I **can** choose to think _about how we'll be together_

for spring break.

I can't change _____

_____

but I can choose to think _____

_____

I can't change _____

_____

but I can choose to think _____

_____

I can't change _____

_____

but I can choose to think _____

_____

I can't change _____

_____

but I can choose to think _____

_____

Find encouraging and soothing QUOTES or THOUGHTS.
Start a collection of the best ones here:

Imagine you are lying on the beach. Waves of emotion wash over you and then recede. Let them come and let them go. What is it like?

Express your
EMOTION
on this page.

Set the

open book

on the

other side

of

the room.

BREATHE.

ELBOW AWARENESS!

Trace or draw your elbow here.

It looks like:

1.

2.

3.

4.

It feels like:

1.

2.

3.

4.

It sounds like:

1.

2.

3.

4.

It smells like:

1.

2.

3.

4.

It tastes like:

1.

2.

3.

4.

I think I'll keep it because:

1.

2.

3.

4.

Top **5 EXTREME** thoughts that trigger your emotional overwhelm:

 1.

 2.

"I can't stand this anymore."

"~~I'll never get this right.~~"

"I will eventually get it – I'll take a break and try again."

"There's not enough time."

"They must hate me."

"I can't handle this."

"No one cares."

3.

4.

5.

"I'll always be alone."

"I feel alone now, but that doesn't mean it will be forever."

Rewrite them from a more accurate viewpoint.

"It's just too hard."

Who are you upset with?

(Including yourself)

NAME: _____

PICTURE:

Try some phrases of forgiveness:

"It's okay, I know you didn't mean it."

"It's okay, we all make mistakes."

"I don't like what happened, but I forgive you."

"Yes, this is a mess, but we can work it out."

"It's okay, nobody's perfect."

Circle any you think you could use.

Write more of your own.

You're a thundercloud about to burst—

what do you need to rain out?

What's your **irrational urge**
right now?

List some actions that are the **opposite** of that.

Choose one and do it.

Circle what feels relaxing for you:

moonlight

swaying palms

sunset

_____

cloudless sky   _____

mountains

frozen tundra

ocean

_____

falling snow

autumn leaves

_____

open meadow

deep forest

_____

beach

_____

sunrise

summer breeze

garden

_____

_____

Close your eyes, breathe quietly, and picture your favorite image. When your mind wanders, simply notice and bring it back. Repeat until you feel peaceful.

MY CURRENT STRUGGLE:

_____

_____

_____

3 POSSIBLE RESPONSES . . .

✳ EMOTIONAL MIND:

"I feel terrible!"
_____

_____

✳ LOGICAL MIND:

"It makes perfect sense that this happened."
_____

_____

✳ WISE MIND:

"The higher meaning of this experience is . . ."

COOL WATER COOL DOWN . . .

a gentle
splash on
the face

wet cloth
on the
back of
your neck

an ice cube
swirling in
your mouth

a
waterfall
in the
shower

bare feet
in a basin

lazy rivulets
down your
inner arm

submerging
in a tub

Try one (or more) and describe your chill.

Picture
of you in
your happy
place:

(where you smile—feel good—
feel joy—get positive energy)

{ What happened
the last time
you were there? }

"I CAN CHOOSE TO LET
IT DEFINE ME, CONFINE
ME, AND OUTSHINE ME,
OR I CAN CHOOSE TO
MOVE ON AND LEAVE
IT BEHIND ME."

—Author Unknown

What would it feel good to leave behind?

Tear out this square and throw it in a dumpster or trashcan far from where you are now. Walk away and don't look back.

LIST THE
PEOPLE YOU
CAN CALL OR
TEXT RIGHT
NOW TO TELL
HOW YOU'RE
FEELING.

PICK ONE
AND DO IT.

Gently place one hand on your heart.

Write to yourself:

" _____, I am here for you.
(your name)

I care about you always."

Repeat.

And again . . .

And again . . .

Tape a picture of something
unfamiliar here.
(people, places, things you know nothing about)

Make up a short story about whatever you see.

Squeeze–Tightly
–and–
Release–Completely

(one at a time, holding to the count of 6)

FOREHEAD

JAW

NECK

SHOULDERS

BICEPS

FOREARMS

HANDS

STOMACH

HIPS

THIGHS

CALVES

FEET

Which . . . relaxed the most?

. . . still feels tense? .

. . . felt really good?

. . . didn't feel good?

. . . tightened the most?

. . . was the hardest to squeeze?

What other muscles would you
add to the list?

"Rollercoaster" thoughts
you're having now:

"Lazy River" thoughts that calm you down:

Close your eyes and take a breath.
Get off the rollercoaster and onto the lazy river ride. Let your
body and mind relax as you float along. How does it feel?

Someone you care about
could use your help.

♥ **NAME:** _____

NEED: _____

WHAT I COULD DO: _____

_____

_____

♥ **NAME:** _____

NEED: _____

WHAT I COULD DO: _____

_____

_____

♥ **NAME:** _____

NEED: _____

WHAT I COULD DO: _____

_____

_____

♥ **NAME:** _____

NEED: _____

WHAT I COULD DO: _____

_____

_____

♥ **NAME:** _____

NEED: _____

WHAT I COULD DO: _____

_____

_____

Reach out to them now.

Gaze into the
flame of a candle.
Follow the dance of the light.
Let your breath soften
and your mind clear.

What thoughts . . .

feelings . . .

behaviors . . .

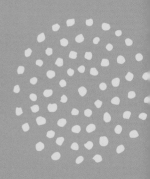

. . . do you need to burn away?

Find – Cut – Arrange – Combine
Glue – Colors – Words
Textures – Pictures – Shapes

Collage your feeling here.

write as much as you can as fast as you can don't think plan organize just let

itallfall
o
c
t

Send your Catastrophic Thoughts

("bad things that might happen") down the drain!

I'll probably fail all my finals.

Rewrite some or all on bathroom tissue. Flush them away!

Now she'll break up with me for sure.

Write a dialogue between

you and your emotion.

Speak with
love and kindness.

Me

Emo

Me

Emo

Me

Emo

Me

What's your dream vacation?

Who you're with . . . What you're doing . . . Place . . . Weather . . . Scenery . . .

Close your eyes and imagine yourself there.

The Ultimate Category Game

CUTE PET NAMES

1
2
3
4
5
6
7
8
9
10

ICE CREAM FLAVORS

1
2
3
4
5
6
7
8
9
10

KIDS' BOARD GAMES

1
2
3
4
5
6
7
8
9
10

TROPICAL DESTINATIONS

1
2
3
4
5
6
7
8
9
10

EXCLAMATIONS
(*EXCLUDING* PROFANITY)

1
2
3
4
5
6
7
8
9
10

PLACES BEGINNING WITH S

1
2
3
4
5
6
7
8
9
10

SHOE STYLES

1
2
3
4
5
6
7
8
9
10

PIZZA TOPPINGS

1
2
3
4
5
6
7
8
9
10

Set a timer for 5 minutes-how many can you complete?

Color the parts

of your body

that are

holding your

emotion

right now.

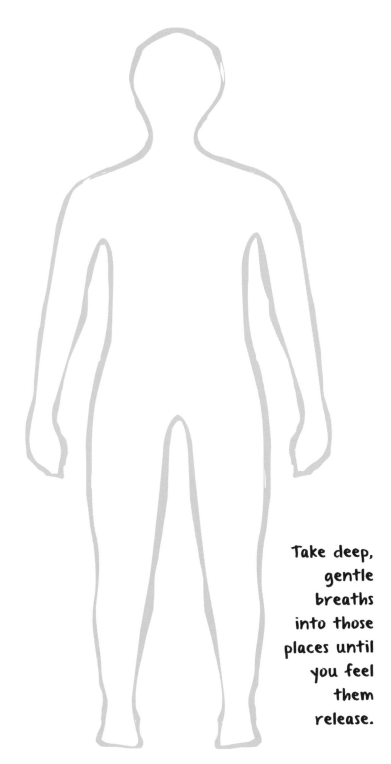

Take deep,
gentle
breaths
into those
places until
you feel
them
release.

DESIGN AN APP FOR MANAGING EMOTION.

Draw your icon here.

launch screen . . .

animations . . .

tasks . . .

features . . .

sound effects . . .

interactions . . .?

Emotional Mind, Logical Mind, and Wise Mind are sitting in a coffee shop talking about your situation. What do they say?

EMOTIONAL MIND

LOGICAL MIND

WISE MIND

What beliefs about

nature   religion   spirituality

the purpose of life   a higher power

give you comfort?

How can you use these beliefs
to help yourself now?

INSIDE:

Create an encouraging greeting card and give it to yourself!

"5 BY 5 RULE: IF IT'S NOT GOING TO MATTER 5 YEARS FROM NOW, DON'T SPEND MORE THAN 5 MINUTES BEING UPSET BY IT."

—Author Unknown

What are you obsessing about?

(Story here.)

Cut it out and let it go.

✂

Breath Break

Comfortable chair. Eyes closed. Find your breath.

Inhale peace . . . exhale stress. . .

. . . inhale peace . . . exhale stress

. . . repeat . . . repeat . . . repeat.

Leave this page blank.

Your emotions are fireworks.
Draw them here. Flaring . . . Flashing . . .
Shimmering . . . Dissolving . . .

Brain Yoga!

Thoughts that create balance: *I am centered in peace.*

_____

_____

Thoughts that increase flexibility: *Imperfection is good enough.*

_____

_____

Thoughts that build strength: *I can tolerate discomfort.*

_____

_____

_____

Write

more that can

help you now.

My 50 Faves:

Friends

Foods

Fun Times

Fashion

Family

131

What do you **usually** do when you feel this way that just <u>makes things worse?</u>

(Explode at someone? Try to escape or numb yourself?

Isolate? Ruminate? Or—?)

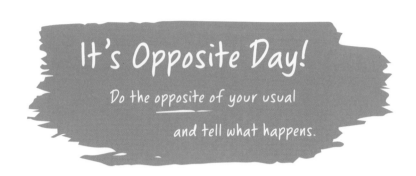

It's Opposite Day!

Do the opposite of your usual ___

and tell what happens.

Mindful Moment with This Journal.

🌿 What the paper feels like when I rub my chin
on it: _____

_____

_____

🌿 What sound it makes when I hit it on the table:

_____

_____

_____

🌿 Do the inside pages smell the same as the cover?

_____

_____

_____

🌿 What I hear when I press my ear to this page:

_____

_____

_____

When I tear off this corner and put it in a glass of water does it dissolve? _____

Can I wrap this book around my arm? _____

How many different fonts are in this book:

_____

(The one I like best:) _____

List of colors in this book: _____

_____

_____

_____

(My favorite: _____)

Other observations: _____

_____

_____

_____

_____

You've got a gift card for the Serenity Shopping Mall. What would you like from each of these stores to help you right now?

Calming Reminders

_____

_____

POSITIVE AFFIRMATIONS

_____

_____

WORDS of WISDOM

_____

_____

STATEMENTS of GRATITUDE

_____

_____

BRIGHT ★ IDEAS

_____

_____

◀◀ UPBEAT IMAGES ▶▶

_____

_____

🍃 Promising Possibilities 🍃

_____

_____

Sunny Perspectives ☀

_____

_____

Give yourself one of these gifts.

WHO'S
YOUR
REAL-LIFE
HERO
AND
WHY?

Are they strong?... Wise? ... Courageous? ...Or ...?

How would they handle the intense emotion

you're feeling right now?

(Try it.)

Stuff your pain
into this box
using words
and pictures.
Leave it there
for a while.

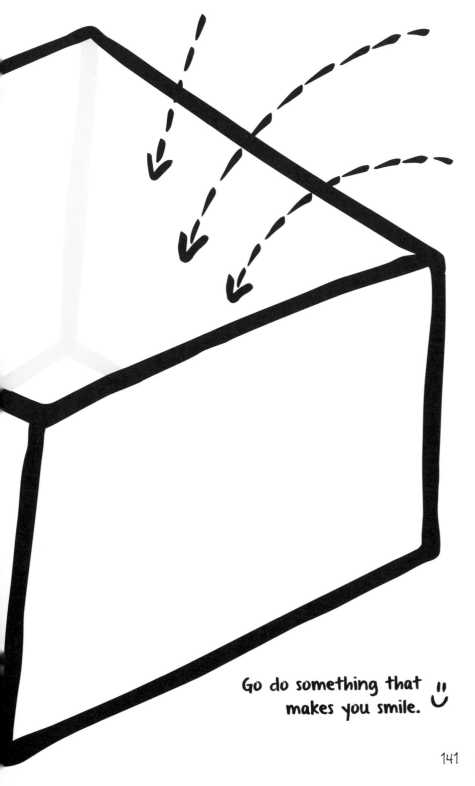

Go do something that makes you smile. ☺

Are you future-tripping?

What thoughts have you packed
that keep you anticipating something
that might never happen?
Come back to the present moment
and keep that suitcase shut.

Close your eyes,

breathe deeply.

Visualize a . . .

setting sun

falling rain

flowing stream

blooming flower

twinkling star

shifting sand dune

or _____

Imagine you can merge into this
natural process and become one with it.
Describe what it's like.

Right now my emotions are urging me to . . .

Instead of acting

on the urge,

I take a breath

. . . and let it pass.

Shoes off.

Socks off.

Walk slowly across 3 different surfaces.

✔ Describe the sensations.

BRAINSTORM!

Your current problem:

Any and all possible solutions:

Try one now!

Your body is made of soft, wide netting. What **thoughts** and **emotions** do you need to let pass through you without getting caught?

153

Draw strong, deep roots grounding this tree. Add words that ground and stabilize you.

Stand firm and balanced, your weight solid over your feet. Feel your body's connection with the earth, continuing down to the center of the planet.

Imagine the situation that's bothering you
is a scene from a movie.

You are cast as the strong, wise hero.

Write the lines the director
would have you say as
you handle it all calmly,
coolly, and effectively.

Pick an ordinary object (Phone? Earring? Paper cup?) and describe it from "Beginner's Mind" (through the eyes of a curious child—as if you've never seen this before.)

* OBJECT *

Do the same for the problem
you're struggling with.

* PROBLEM *

"WHEN YOU REACT, YOU LET OTHERS CONTROL YOU. WHEN YOU RESPOND, YOU ARE IN CONTROL."

—Bohdi Sanders

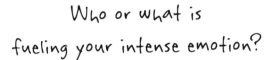

Who or what is
fueling your intense emotion?

_____

Don't let something outside
yourself run your life.
How could you respond differently
to take back your control?

_____

_____

_____

_____

You're sitting in the very back row

What thoughts are on the screen right now?

of your mind's movie theater.

Imagine (or draw) yourself leaving the theater.
What happens?

Inhale . . . Exhale . . . Trace . . .

thick . . . thin . . . dotted . . . dashed . . .
squiggly . . . spiraly . . . wavy . . . ink . . .
pencil . . . crayon . . . lines

ATHE

Write notes to the person you're upset with (it could be you . . .)

1. FROM EMOTIONAL MIND

2. FROM LOGICAL MIND

3. FROM WISE MIND

If you need more space,
tape extra paper here.

Draw yourself walking easily across this
TIGHTROPE. On the balancing pole you're
holding, list the thoughts that keep you steady.

Create the **ID card** for what you're feeling right now . . .

NAME, DATE, PICTURE, INTENSITY, ORIGIN,
CURRENT LOCATION, SIGNATURE . . .

Relocate—Regroup!

Leave wherever you are right now.

(Bring this book with you.)

Put yourself in a new place . . .

take a new breath . . .

clear your mind.

Write new thoughts

from a new perspective.

scented candle

fresh mint

cut grass

clean laundry

cookies baking

pine trees

cologne or perfume

coffee brewing

eucalyptus

fresh flowers

fresh air

Find a calming scent and breathe it in from your nose to your toes. Then put it into words...

Find 10 synonyms for "calm."

Write something about yourself using each of them.

1.

2.

3.

4.

5.

6.

7.

8.

9.

10.

Sift a handful of sand or salt
back and forth slowly through your fingers.
Let it fall randomly on a flat surface.

Recreate part of the pattern here. . .

or write about what you see.

"EMOTIONAL
INTELLIGENCE IS THE
ABILITY TO MAKE
EMOTIONS WORK FOR
YOU INSTEAD OF
AGAINST YOU. "

—Justin Bariso

Imagine there's a safe place
deep at the center
of your being.
What would it
look and feel
like?

Close your eyes and connect with it now.

PAST

Thoughts about the **PAST** that are triggering my emotions:

PRESENT MOMENT:
date ... time ... season ...
my age ... who I'm with ...
where I am ... the weather ...
what I'm wearing ... what
I'm doing.

Thoughts about the **FUTURE** that are setting me off:

Use opaque tape to

PRESENT MOMENT

FUTURE

cover up anything that is not happening NOW.

***** Plan Your ***** ULTIMATE PARTY
(no limits!)

* Guest List

* Location

* Music

✳ Food

✳ Decorations

✳ Entertainment

✴ More

Intense emotion can hurt.
You don't need more pain.

List 10 things you could do to be kind to
yourself instead of hurting yourself more.

1 _____

_____

2 _____

_____

3 _____

_____

4 _____

_____

5 _____

_____

6 _____

_____

7 _____

_____

8 _____

_____

9 _____

_____

10 _____

_____

Try one now!

Design a gentle STOPP sign for yourself.

Stop what you're doing.

Take a breath.

Observe: How are you acting? Thinking? Feeling?

Pause for another breath, and . . .

Proceed, acting from Wise Mind.

Switch from OMG

to **LOL.**

(Describe your situation
as if it were a comedy.)

Something to look forward
to in the next:

DAY

WEEK

MONTH

YEAR

(If you think there's nothing,
create something and tell how
you can make it happen!)

Your mind's
Thought Machine
has two conveyor belts.
Label one "Keep" and
one "Let Go." Write your
current thoughts on the
belts of your choice.

Put a picture or symbol of something peaceful in the center of this page.

Sit comfortably, breathe slowly . . . gaze at the picture until your emotional storm subsides.

Write what
you've been holding in.

Then make
confetti out of this page!

WHAT TO DO NEXT

After you've completed all the prompts that you'd like to, take a look back at your emotional intensity chart from the beginning of the book. If you filled it out, see what you notice about your answers. If there are certain prompts or types of prompts that seemed to help you reduce intense emotions the most, write them here:

_____   _____

_____   _____

_____   _____

_____   _____

_____   _____

_____   _____

_____   _____

If you didn't fill out the chart—or even if you did—you can flip back through this book and put stars on any of the pages that you enjoyed or that helped you the most.

Think about whether the most helpful
prompts had to do with:

breath work
distracting yourself
mindfulness
working with thoughts
soothing yourself
physically releasing emotion
practicing acceptance
separating from emotions
separating from thoughts
using wise mind
relaxing your body
problem-solving
Or?

_____

_____

_____

REMEMBER THIS (REALLY IMPORTANT):

If you had any success at all—even the tiniest bit— in regulating your emotions, you are the one who made it happen. (Not the person who gave you the book, the person who wrote the book, or the prompts themselves.) It was *your actions* that lowered your emotional intensity. *This is important to remember because it means you have the ability to calm yourself down.* That is a really powerful skill that you carry with you at every moment. No matter where you are, who you're with, or what you're doing, you can use the resources inside you to self–regulate.

Go gently into the future. Now that you recognize your ability, it will take time and practice to become proficient at using it. Be patient. Try new ways and tweak your processes over and over until you find what works best. Be assured that you are headed in the right direction and will eventually arrive at the very place you need to be.

Write your own prompt here:

Note to parents, professionals, and anyone caring for an emotional teen:

Put Your Feelings Here offers 100 journaling prompts designed specifically to help teens release and reduce intense emotions *in the moment.* Creative, engaging, and clinically based, the prompts are grounded in the principles of dialectical behavioral therapy as well as cognitive behavioral therapy, mindfulness-based therapies, and neuroscience.

The journal can be used by a teen on their own, or as an adjunct to counseling or psychotherapy. It lends itself both to individual and group settings and can help the average adolescent as well as the hard-to-reach teen and those uncomfortable with traditional talk therapy.

Where direct questioning and exploration might feel threatening, journaling prompts are more subtle and can bypass defenses. When used at times of intense emotion, the journal can help to interrupt the habitual behavior cycle, decrease overwhelming affect, and allow the teen to respond thoughtfully instead of reacting impulsively to the triggering situation. Prompts are designed to help teens self-soothe through techniques such as breathwork, distraction and refocusing, mindfulness, working with thought patterns, identification and acceptance of emotions, and physical release. Creative prompts help teens identify emotional triggers, develop coping skills, and regulate emotion while still maintaining comfort with the process.

For a clinical guide to using this book specifically, and journaling as an adjunct to therapy in general, please visit http://www.lisamschabooks.com. Alternatively, you can visit http://www.newharbinger.com/44239 and follow the instructions there to register your book and download the companion guide. If you are interested in earning continuing education credits for Lisa Schab's courses on journaling as an adjunct to therapy, please visit https://www.pdresources.org/.

Acknowledgments

My heartfelt thanks to my "teammates": Tesilya Hanauer, Clancy Drake, Amy Shoup, and Michele Waters, whose excellent contributions, input, and energy have made this book shine. Many thanks to all the staff at New Harbinger Publications who help me in so many ways throughout the creation and marketing of each book. And thanks, again, to Amy Blue, who finds what I need every time!